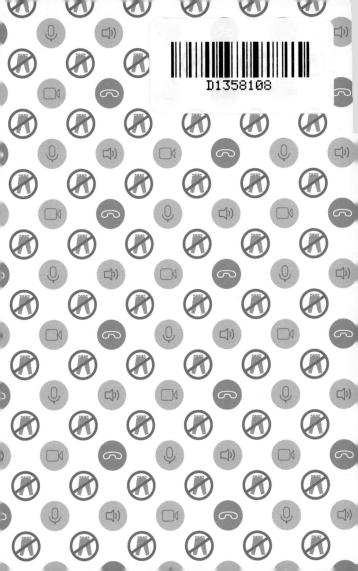

I'M NOT WEARING
ANY
TROUSERS

AND OTHER WORKING FROM HOME TRUTHS

ABBIE HEADON

HarperCollins*Publishers*

HarperCollins*Publishers*
1 London Bridge Street
London SE1 9GF

www.harpercollins.co.uk

First published by HarperCollins*Publishers* 2020

1 3 5 7 9 10 8 6 4 2

Text © HarperCollins*Publishers* 2020
Illustrations © Shutterstock.com

Abbie Headon asserts the moral right to
be identified as the author of this work

A catalogue record of this book is
available from the British Library

ISBN 978-0-00-845873-7

Printed and bound in Great Britain by
CPI Group (UK) Ltd, Croydon

MIX
Paper from
responsible sources
FSC™ C007454

This book is produced from independently certified FSC™ paper
to ensure responsible forest management.

For more information visit: www.harpercollins.co.uk/green

WARNING

FOR OPTIMAL ENJOYMENT, NO TROUSERS SHOULD BE WORN WHILE READING THIS BOOK.

CONTENTS

INTRODUCTION

———————⟨K⟩———————

Welcome to *I'm Not Wearing Any Trousers*, the ultimate working from home survival guide!

Since a certain virus made its presence felt in early 2020, business life has changed for most of us in office jobs. Instead of getting dressed and going to work every day, we're more likely to tumble out of bed, stumble to the kitchen and then just stay there all day hunched over a laptop, drinking more cups of ambition★ than are strictly good for us.

Working from home can be a lot more fun than the boring old office slog. As you'll already know from picking up this book, trousers are now entirely optional – as long as you maintain an illusion of

---

★ Coffee, obviously – 'ambition' feels a bit, well, *ambitious* to those of us sitting in the pyjamas we were sleeping in last night. And the night before. And … well, you get the picture.

professionalism from the waist up, your boss and customers will be satisfied. And it's not just your trousers that you can consign to the dustbin of history; you can say *au revoir* to tedious commuting, *auf Wiedersehen* to awkward small talk while you're waiting for the kettle to boil and *sayonara* to queuing for the photocopier.

Of course, it's not *all* plain sailing here in WFH-land. After all, commuting gives you an excuse to sit down with a good book before starting work (not you, drivers – unless it's an audiobook, of course), kitchen conversations can be the best sources of office gossip and when you're WFH there actually isn't a photocopier, which is occasionally quite inconvenient, as it turns out. But still: no trousers trumps all of this.

WELCOME TO THE CLUB

This book is designed to welcome newbie WFH-ers into the world of optional trouserage, to celebrate everything that makes life at home more fun than the daily grind in the office, and to give you tips on how to Zoom like a total boss, win the obligatory Friday Quiz and basically get through the day without showing all your colleagues that you are, in fact, trouserless.

Whether you're a recent convert to WFH or a long-term freelance hermit, you are welcome here – fun, flexibility, unlimited snack breaks and stretchy clothes await you! You'll be a pro in no time. And you never need to wear trousers ever again.

WORKING
-FROM-HOMERS,
UNITE!

YOU HAVE NOTHING TO LOSE BUT YOUR:

- SOCIAL SKILLS

- CURRENT CLOTHES SIZE

- ABILITY TO DRESS SMARTLY
  BELOW WAIST LEVEL

WORKING FROM HOME

YOUR TIMETABLE FOR THE DAY

A common problem of the WFH lifestyle is that time loses its structure, and every day (heck, every hour) can feel much the same as the one before. So boss your day from sun-up to sun-downer with this handy timetable.

7:00 A.M. *Your alarm goes off. You remember you don't have to wear smart clothes, do your make-up or commute anywhere. Back to sleep!*

8:00 A.M. *OK, it's probably time to think about getting up now. Sorry about that. You'll want to plan your outfit of the day. No meetings? Might as well stay in your pyjamas. Big presentation to the board? Time to dig out that shirt and jacket you last wore in February 2020. You've got this!*

9:00 A.M. *Better crank up the computer and find out what delights are waiting in your inbox.*

9:05 A.M. *COFFEE BREAK ☕ (you don't want to rush things, after all).*

9:30 A.M. *Plan the day, answer an email or two, WhatsApp your work BFF.*

10:00 A.M. *Company meeting: time to break out your 'interested employee' face. Don't worry, it won't last too long. And then you can have another …*

10:30 A.M. *COFFEE BREAK* ☕

11:00 A.M. *Time to get some work done.*

12:00 P.M. *LUNCH BREAK* 🍱 *(well done for holding out so long, you hero).*

1:00 P.M. *EXERCISE: you could theoretically still be at lunch, so you might as well take a spin round the park for an hour. If anyone asks, you're brainstorming new ideas, thinking blue-sky thoughts and shifting paradigms, even if it looks like you're just feeding the pigeons.*

2:00 P.M. *One-to-one meeting. You can tell your boss about that email you sent this morning. Nice going!*

3:00 P.M. *COFFEE BREAK* ☕ *(you're allowed to switch to tea if you're getting a bit twitchy).*

3:30 P.M. *Time to get some more work done (maybe).*

4:00 P.M. *COFFEE BREAK* ☕ *(you'll definitely need biscuits with this).*

4:30 P.M.   *The Big Presentation. No, I don't know why it was scheduled for the end of the day, either. Can't the international office get up earlier, FFS?*

5:30 P.M.   *Pens down everyone – it's time to stop and have a GIN BREAK* 🍸

... UNLESS ...

6:00 P.M.   *The Work Social, aka Enforced Fun*

7:00 P.M.   *UNPLUG (not really, just stare at your phone on the sofa while also watching TV).*

LATER   *Sleep – no honestly, this will be fine, it's not as if you've been indoors nearly all day, staring at screens of varying sizes, feeling stressed, with no colleagues to bitch with in the kitchen over coffee, you'll fall asleep just like that* 👀

Read on, brave WFH-er, as we venture into the ups and downs of the non-office day. All of the advice in the following chapters has been scientifically researched★ to help get you through the WFH day while screaming 'WTF?!' as little as possible.

★ No science, research or trousers were involved.

STARTING THE DAY

It's important to re-create that commuting-to-work vibe as authentically as possible if you're going to start the WFH day in a truly professional frame of mind. This handy guide will get you in the right mood, so you turn up to the office (i.e. to your desk/kitchen table) feeling properly stressed, frazzled and grumpy. *Bon voyage!*

IT'S NOT GOOD TO TALK

For the best start to your WFH commute, make an agreement with your housemates, partner and/or family members not to talk or smile before 9:30 a.m. There, that's better.

BREAKFAST

Obviously when you're commuting you don't have time for a peaceful breakfast at the kitchen table, so you'll need to take this most important meal of the day on your journey. You'll need the following ingredients:

* An expensive but somewhat mediocre coffee, served either far too hot or much too cold. For the full experience, stand in line waiting to get your coffee until you're almost too late for work, while another member of your household stands in front of you hunting slowly and inefficiently for their loyalty card ('I'm sure it's in here somewhere, let me just check the other pocket …').
* A croissant, baked yesterday but sold to you today for at least £2.00.
* If no stale pastries are available, a small Tupperware container of muesli will do instead. Or a chocolate bar (your WFH day, your rules).

For a proper commuting breakfast you'll need to hold your cup and food item of choice as well as a bag containing everything you'll need for the day, while wearing all your outdoor clothes. A wet umbrella clasped to your side is a bonus, and if any helpful housemates can jog your elbow just as you're about to sip your lava-hot coffee, so much the better.

Ideally by the end of breakfast you'll be too hot, you'll have coffee stains and/or pastry crumbs on your coat and shoes, and you'll be down at least a fiver. Good work!

RE: CYCLING

You could go out for a cycle before starting work, getting some fresh air and sunshine (or daylight, at least) into the start of your day. But if you want to be true to the ethics of WFH, there is another way.

YOU WILL NEED

* Your old exercise bike. Can't find it? Remember, it's in the bedroom, under a huge pile of washing. Just remove a few more layers and you'll find it. Careful not to choke on the dust – you haven't used it in a while.
* A full set of outdoor clothes, including waterproof trousers (don't worry – you can go back to wearing no trousers as soon as you get to work).
* A heavy bag, either dangling precariously from one shoulder or hanging from your handlebar.
* A spray bottle full of water, dirty if possible.

METHOD

* Try to make sure the bike is positioned in a tight spot so you feel you're constantly in danger of being squashed or falling off.
* Set up a playlist of engine noise, car horns and (this one's just for the female cyclists) sudden shouted sexual remarks.
* Climb aboard your bike, feeling flustered because you're running late.
* Ask a member of your household to spray you with dirty water just when you're not expecting it. A face-shot will get you in the perfect mood for a day in the office.

If you follow these instructions for at least twenty minutes, you should arrive at work hot, sweaty, scared and enraged. No time for a shower – proceed directly to your first meeting of the day. There's really nothing like a refreshing cycle ride, is there?

RECREATE THE STRAIN OF THE TRAIN

For the ultimate peak-time railway experience you'll want to be nicely squashed, and alternately too hot and too cold. If you don't have access to total strangers for this part of the journey, see if you can persuade any spouses, housemates, children or pets to take up all your personal space (something which is often not a problem with the two latter groups anyway). Squeeze into your shower cubicle wearing your boots, coat, woolly hat and scarf, and sway from side to side while listening to someone else's terrible music from the outside of their headphones.

If you don't have a shower cubicle, an airing cupboard is a great alternative and creates an authentic 'stuck in a Tube tunnel in the dark for longer than seems reasonable' vibe that can't be matched anywhere else in your home.

Make-up wearers: this is your chance to practise your artistic skills, recreating the uneven wobbly eyeliner you're known for. If there's nobody around to jog your arm as you're pointing a brush laden with make-up

FEELING RELAXED?

THEN YOU'RE DOING IT WRONG.

directly at your eyeball, you can sit on the washing machine during its spin cycle for a very similar effect. (Any other effects of this manoeuvre on your mood are somewhat outside the scope of this book.)

Washing machines aside, with this journey technique you should emerge grumpier and slightly more dishevelled than you started, with an attractive fresh-from-the-Tube sheen – just the way to begin the day.

BUSRIDER'S HOLIDAY

The instructions for a WFH bus commute are largely similar to the train tips above, but for this one you'll need sudden jolts left, right, forwards and backwards as you're travelling. Ideally you'll want to step on someone's foot *and* have someone step on yours.

If you can arrange for a damp backpack to be pressed into your face while a polite robotic voice explains that there are 91 more stops before you reach your destination, so much the better. You'll definitely find it impossible to read more than two pages of your book under these circumstances, and that's the main thing.

DRIVING YOURSELF BANANAS

You don't have to join the herd and save the environment for your WFH commute – you can always drive instead. For this variant you'll need to tie yourself into an armchair for half an hour while listening to the news, becoming increasingly outraged at how useless everyone who's supposed to be in charge is at their jobs and worrying about what the day will bring.

If you can set up a TV or computer screen to show a boring motorway or (even better) an unmoving scene of packed traffic, that will bring more verité and stress to the experience.

OPTIONAL PARENTING ADD-ON

If you have children you can add extra depth to your WFH commute:

Ask your children to sing the same song over and over. In fact you probably won't even have to ask them – they'll know in advance this is helpful, and they'll choose the least restful song. If in doubt, 'Let It Go' from *Frozen* is a sure-fire winner.

Arrange for your children to start arguing about who saw something outside the window first – this will prepare you for workplace conversations about who had the idea for the new product design first. Lovely.

If possible, make sure one of your children shouts, 'I need a poo NOW' and then says, 'No, it's OK' and goes ominously quiet for the next ten minutes.

WALK LIKE A COMMUTER

Obviously walking to your WFH job is the most peaceful option of all the commuting methods, so only do this if none of the options above are available, or you'll risk being far too chilled to appreciate the urgent spreadsheets and high-pressure virtual meetings that are awaiting you today.

If you *must* go outside, try to choose a route with as much traffic as possible, or, even better, play yourself a soundtrack of car and bus horns so you feel genuinely stressed by the time you get home again.

An alternative for those of us who've stayed true to the trouserless goals of WFH is to pace around your home, dodging piles of papers from work (you said you were going to look into them, you optimistic star-child, but now you know better) and that mini scooter your offspring left helpfully at the top of the stairs. A hundred or so circuits of the front room should get you nicely tuned in to the sheer futility of whatever the day has in store.

Remember, if you start your WFH day feeling calm, well-fed and as if you've just rolled out of bed, you're going to be in much too good a mood to face your first virtual meeting – and we all know that being too cheerful in meetings can lead to suddenly being given extra work to do. Nobody wants that. Never skimp on these stages or you might end up feeling relaxed and mellow for the rest of the day.

AGONY AUNT LETTER

'Dear WFH Agony Aunt, I get that feeling stressed and sweaty is important, but I'd like to use my bonus non-commuting time to do something nice instead. Isn't that a good idea?

Yours, Hopelessly Optimistic and New to All This WFH Malarkey'

Well, yes, Hopelessly Optimistic, there are loads of things you could do with an extra hour at the start and end of each day. You could write that novel you've been banging on about – no, please, the world needs more novels, really it does. You could go for a jog, tend to your sourdough starter, take up t'ai chi. You could even give yourself an extra lie-in.

But if you truly want to be in the right frame of mind for a day at work, what you need is an hour scrolling through Twitter and Instagram, ideally losing your Wi-Fi signal every few minutes, while standing up and holding a cup of expensive coffee. By the time you start work you'll be so cross about the state of the world and jealous of how much fun everyone else seems to be having that you'll be typing passive–aggressive emails like a pro.

THE PERFECT
WFH OFFICE

In the new era of long-term WFH there's no boundary between work and home any more – it all happens in the same place. This means you can design the perfect workspace just for you, at least as far as your space and budget will allow, and you don't have to stare at grey carpet, grey walls and grey ceiling tiles all day long (unless your home décor is based on a vision of 'soulless office chic').

Some people say an Englishman's home is his castle. We say a WFH-er's home is their office. So whether you live in a castle or a flatshare, it's time to make your office as castle-like as possible.

ALL HOME OFFICES GREAT AND SMALL

If you don't have a full castle at your disposal, you'll probably need to repurpose a space for your home office that you were previously using for something else. Let's take a tour of the pros and cons of the most popular workspaces:

BED

FOR: Literally the shortest possible commute to work; exceptionally cosy; your teddy bear can stand in for you in online meetings if you're busy.

AGAINST: Probably the hardest WFH space to stay awake in; having to answer the question 'Are you still in *bed?!?*' several times a day.

DINING TABLE

FOR: Nice and spacious, probably only needs to be cleared at the end of the day so everyone can eat.

AGAINST: Dining rooms are the loneliest places when it's not dinner time. Your housemates may forget you exist – heck, *you* may forget you exist. Best to set up a reminder so someone can check you haven't died from time to time.

KITCHEN TABLE	**FOR:** Best location for regular access to snacks; other household members will be in and out through the day so you won't get lonely.	**AGAINST:** Best location for regular access to snacks; other household members will be in and out through the day so you won't get anything done.
SOFA	**FOR:** Second-comfiest location after your bed; ideal for dual-screening the daily soaps on the TV while you're answering emails on your laptop.	**AGAINST:** Your back may never forgive you after a week or two; unplanned naps can sneak up on you during meetings. 'Samantha, what are your thoughts on the proposal? Samantha? ARE YOU ASLEEP? Ah, you're back with us. You might want to wipe that dribble off your cheek.'
ATTIC	**FOR:** Remote and peaceful; ideal for getting away from distractions (e.g. the view from a window).	**AGAINST:** Spiders and mice for company (though this can be a 'for', depending on your tastes); you'll never get down to the front door in time to retrieve your parcels.

SHED

FOR: Allows you to truthfully say 'I'm going to work' when you start the working day, as it's not actually in your home; lets you get in touch with nature.

AGAINST: Usually too cold, otherwise too hot; tends to be full of hazards such as precariously balanced paint pots and jars of nails; not great for broadband connectivity (though again, this can be a plus if you're sick of endless meetings).

TENT

FOR: Allows you to work anywhere; nice and bright; lets you feel smug about getting away from it all while still doing your job.

AGAINST: Risk of being blown away during a conference call; may be cold enough to require trousers, thus negating the key plus-point of WFH in the first place.

WFH?

I THINK YOU MEAN

WFB!

SUMMER IN THE CITY (AND THE SUBURBS, AND ALL OTHER WFH LOCATIONS)

When you're melting in your home workspace on a hot summer's day, you just *know* a well-meaning relative will pipe up with the following: 'Oh, how lovely, you can work outside in the summer!'

Yes, because it's just great when you:

* can't see your screen because the sun is too bright.
* are surrounded by bees, wasps and other things with wings and stings.
* have to be constantly on your guard against stray footballs (why can't parks be kept just for workers? It's really not fair).
* get sunburnt while you're trying to understand clause 19.2 subsection 7 of an important contract.

* are exposed to a soundtrack of other people's summer party music.
* have to smell the tantalising aromas of someone else's barbecue.

Seriously, even if it means taking off not just your trousers but everything else as well, you're likely to get much more done if you just stay indoors.

I WANT TO BE ALONE

If your housemates are driving you to distraction and you can't stand sharing the kitchen table with them any more, try these alternative micro-offices for a change:

* **GIANT CARDBOARD BOX**: see, those online orders were useful after all!
* **AIRING CUPBOARD**: just make sure someone comes to check on you before you dry out completely.

* **BALCONY:** take a break from contemplating the endless supply of emails in your inbox to contemplate the traffic outside for a bit instead.
* **BATH TUB:** an unusual choice but very secluded if you have a shower curtain. You might want to let your housemates know you've there, to avoid hearing more of their habits than you ever wanted to.

WHAT YOU WANT YOUR CO-WORKERS TO SEE …

Working from home gives you the opportunity to curate the perfect online-meeting backdrop to impress your colleagues. Anything that doesn't fit your artistic vision can rest out of sight on the other side of your laptop screen – so, while you might be staring at a heap of slowly fermenting washing, you can relax in the knowledge that your co-workers can only see what you want them to see.

As well as showing off your skills and your impeccable taste, the objects you choose might just confuse your boss into talking about something other than your KPIs and the fact that you've failed to meet them yet again – so it's win–win.

LARGE ABSTRACT PAINTING

Make sure you position yourself to one side of your camera, so people have the best view of your masterwork. When questioned, remain nonchalant: 'Oh, this. Yes, it's one of a series of canvasses representing my creative journey, building on the tragedies of Aeschylus – oh, you're not familiar with his works? Well, let me explain …'

If you don't have an artwork of your own to display, try printing off one of your favourite works of art and framing it. 'Oh, this. I inherited it.'

SPORTS TROPHY

'Oh, that old thing. Well, it's nothing really, just a memento of my days as an Oxford Blue/Olympic triathlete/international Scrabble champion. I mean, it's probably not relevant to this meeting, but I suppose it all started back in my school days when I was chosen for the inter-county team …'

UNIDENTIFIABLE CLAY OBJECT

'Yes, that was made by my youngest – she really does have such an eye for three-dimensional form … It's really all about the negative space, and there are clear parallels with Barbara Hepworth, as I'm sure you'll agree. David, are you still there …?'

FRAMED CERTIFICATE

It's unlikely anyone will be able to zoom in too closely, so practise turning slowly in your chair and repeating the words, 'Oh, that. It's just my doctorate,' while glancing at your 20m front-crawl certificate. You worked hard for that!

... AND WHAT YOU DON'T

Remember, you're not wearing any trousers, so you'll need to arrange your WFH space so it only shows you from the waist up. For safety's sake, and to avoid getting HR on your case, attach a Post-it to your laptop screen showing the following warning sign:

Then whenever you stand up you'll remember to tilt your laptop screen too. Phew!

REALITY

WHAT THEY SEE

OTHER THINGS TO AVOID SHOWING IN YOUR WFH CAMERA VIEW

* **DEAD PLANTS:** it might be tricky convincing your colleagues you're able to run your department if you can't even keep a spider plant alive.

* **CLOTHES AIRER DRAPED IN PANTS AND SOCKS:** though at least this does demonstrate that you're probably wearing clean pants and socks.

* **SEX TOYS:** unless of course you work for a company that supplies such furnishings and you want to show your boss how committed you are to next season's collection.

WINNING AT ONLINE MEETINGS

Before WFH became the norm for millions of us, 'online video conferencing' was something that happened on special occasions, to talk to an important client on another continent or watch a presentation from the Big Boss to all the global teams. But not now. Oh no – now online meetings are part of our daily lives, enabling us to admire the MD's mansion while also showing off our own multipurpose living/working/eating/crying spaces to our colleagues.

HACK THE PROCESS

Virtual meetings may be a non-negotiable part of our home-office lives now, but that doesn't mean we can't show them who's boss. These meeting hacks will see you emerging from the departmental video call like a true champ.

Other participants disagreeing with your proposal? Passive–aggressively pretend the sound is playing up, to get your way. 'I can't really hear what Jen is saying, but I'm pretty sure she prefers the blue version, right Jen? Great! Let's move on,' as Jen screams 'THE RED ONE, YOU £$C!" £$%✶✶'

Before the meeting begins, send bingo cards round to your closest office allies and compete to tick the boxes whenever you see someone:

- ☐ yawning
- ☐ picking their nose
- ☐ daydreaming
- ☐ making audible 'clacks' with their dry mouth when they talk
- ☐ trying to suppress a burp
- ☐ dozing
- ☐ playing on their phone
- ☐ eating

- ☐ slurping
- ☐ smelling their own armpits and reacting
- ☐ putting their head in their hands in despair at what their life has become

Try not to shout 'HOUSE!' when your bingo card is full – unless you're competing with a colleague, that is.

Practise breathing techniques to help you overcome your impulse to howl with frustration every time you hear the words, 'Sorry, I was on mute.'

If somebody asks you a question and you don't know the answer, stay very still and pretend your screen has frozen. Out of shot, slowly reach for the mouse and hang up. The trick here is not to move your eyes.

Position your face out of sight of your laptop camera and send a hand puppet to deputise for you instead. If anyone challenges you, explain that it's an innovative new business technique.

AND THE OSCAR FOR BEST GREEN SCREEN GOES TO ...

If all your attempts to create an Instagram-worthy home office have failed, and you realise that your laptop camera is pointing at a kitchen sink full of unwashed dishes and a falling-down light fitting, then your meeting software's green-screen feature is your new BFF. Instead of showing your colleagues your collection of *Star Wars*-themed Hello Kittys or your poster of Mona Lisa smoking a joint, you can set a professional tone for your important meetings with one of the following virtual backgrounds:

* interior of the Death Star
* Alcatraz prison cell
* 'ABANDON HOPE ALL YE WHO ENTER HERE' sign
* cheerful 'Don't Panic!' sign with the 'Don't' crossed out
* desert plain with rolling tumbleweed
* toxic waste dump

WARNING: although your green screen will make your surroundings invisible, it won't make *you* invisible, so you will still need to check whether you're modelling an 'I woke up like this – because I've literally just woken up' look before logging in.

MEETING FAILS

There is, alas, no international convention defining which behaviours are acceptable in online meetings, but we all know from painful experience what our own bugbears are. If you spot any of the following crimes against workplace humanity, feel free to send a strongly worded letter to the UN, or failing that, a really bitchy direct message to your online backchannel.

(If you find yourself doing any of these, it is of course totally understandable and everyone just needs to chill out a little, OK?)

ONLINE MEETING CRIMES

A household member enters the room, says hello, realises there's a meeting on, and says slowly and loudly, 'OH SORRY, I DIDN'T KNOW YOU WERE IN A MEETING' while walking backwards through the door.

A child enters the room and tries to get their parent's attention, eventually climbing onto the parent's lap and facepalming them or pulling their hair.

A person's housemate comes into the room without enough clothes on.

Someone participating in the meeting stands up and reveals they only got dressed from the waist up today. A bonus guardian-angel point to the first person who shouts, 'Martin, your camera is on!'

A cat jumps on the person's desk and positions itself so all present can enjoy a close-up view of its arsehole.

You stare at your own face for so long that you lose track of what anyone else is saying.

Someone shares their screen and reveals bookmarked web pages for ineedanewjob.com and literallyanyjobwoulddo.com.

A colleague's camera is angled/positioned to show a detailed view of their nostrils and/or multiple chins.

Someone places their hand so close to the camera that all you can see is one terrifying giant waggling thumb and you can't concentrate on anything else.

WHAT TO SAY WHEN YOU'RE BUSY ON TWITTER AND YOU'RE SUDDENLY ASKED A QUESTION

'I'm so glad you asked that!' (pause – with luck they'll repeat the question)

'Interesting. Before I start, I wonder if you have anything to add, Dave?'

'Let's look at this another way – can you find a new angle on this question, Felicia?'

'You know, I'd really love to know what you think about this first?'

'Sorry, I was lost in thought about the next strategy away day – these big ideas just won't wait!'

'Hmmmm. I was meditating on the company mission statement and didn't get that last bit. Can you be more specific?'

WHAT TO DO WHEN NATURE CALLS DURING A TWO-HOUR ZOOM MEETING

It happens to us all: you're sitting there, enduring yet another discussion about the reallocation of fixed costs, and your body tells you that that litre of coffee you inhaled just to be able to fake alertness during the meeting is now ready to leave your body. And it's not prepared to wait another minute.

Here are some handy techniques to help you out of this urgent situation:

Say, 'Sorry, I have to get some important figures from the other room,' go and have the best wee of your life, then come back clutching some sheets of A4 (just try not to let anyone see that they're blank).

If you need to keep abreast of what's going on, switch off your camera, sneak off to the bathroom while still listening to the discussion and then switch it back on again, trying not to look too obviously relieved. NB, you do need to turn off your microphone too or you won't fool anyone.

For the most work-obsessed, you can simply keep a potty under your work desk, but again, you'll need to be very thorough with the mute button (though your trouserless state should make things easier). And if your workspace is somewhere communal like the kitchen table, be prepared for your housemates to react with dismay to your hyper-efficient time-saving techniques.

THE ALL-DAY VIDEO CONFERENCE: A VIEW FROM THE PSYCHIATRIST'S COUCH

You may think your all-day online conference is just another day at the WFH coalface, but what you're experiencing is known in psychiatric circles as the Five Stages of Grief:

DENIAL: *'Surely it's not only 10 a.m.? And I have to get through another seven hours of this? This can't be happening to me. What did I do in a past life to deserve this? Whatever it was, I'm sorry, OK?'*

ANGER: *'I cannot believe I have to listen to all this. No, seriously, if I have to look at your faces for just ONE MORE MINUTE I'm going to –'*

BARGAINING: *'If I have a biscuit and a cup of tea every half-hour I might just make it through this.'*

DEPRESSION: *'It's still only 11 a.m., I've eaten all the biscuits and this meeting is never going to end. And now I really need a wee after all that tea.'*

ACCEPTANCE: *'If I can fake a mildly interested expression for the rest of the day and manage not to swear in front of everyone, I'm going to count this as a win.'*

If you're really lucky, you'll get to experience this cycle every few weeks. It never gets any easier. The only way to make it stop is to quit your job, 'accidentally' cut your broadband cable in a freak home DIY incident, become a hermit, or all three at once just to be on the safe side.

1	2	3	4	5
Denial	Anger	Bargaining	Depression	Acceptance

THINGS YOU NEVER WANT TO HEAR DURING AN ONLINE MEETING

A loud 'splosh', followed by a satisfied groan and prolonged flushing.

'Yes, my poppet? Is it a Number One or a Number Two? Or both? Oh, lovely.'

'Mark, I think the dog's going to be – oh no! Can you bring a wet cloth and a bucket?'

Your colleague's offspring's violin practice.

Seagulls and ice cream van jingles – how dare anyone be having a better time than you (and no wonder their camera is switched off at the moment)?

'Yes, like that, yes, just a little more, don't stop, YES, LIKE THAT, YESSSS, OH GOD!'

IT NEVER ENDS

After a long day of meetings, there's nothing like unwinding and meeting up with a selection of friends and family members to chew the fat. With times being as they are, in-person meet-ups aren't always practical, so it's time to fire up the laptop again for another few hours of staring at your own increasingly exhausted face, reminding Aunty Sandra to unmute and hearing about your best friend's horrific day of back-to-back virtual meetings. So relaxing …

EMAILING LIKE A BOSS

You can't spend *all* your time in online meetings, even though it does feel that way sometimes. But luckily for you, WFH means that when you're not losing the will to live staring at your colleagues' interior-design choices, you can be losing the will to live staring at your colleagues' emails instead.

EMAIL ENGLISH 101

The English language seems deceptively simple and easy to use, especially for those of us who've been speaking it for decades, but when deployed in 12pt Arial in an email window it can be rapidly weaponised. In the hands of a skilled email tactician, even the most outwardly polite of phrases can have the impact of a 100-decibel tirade of swearwords.

COMPANY INBOXES
BORED AND EMPTY?

"REPLY ALL"

FORMULA IS
GUARANTEED
TO FILL 'EM UP AGAIN

WHAT YOU TYPE	WHAT YOU ACTUALLY MEAN
As per my last email	You ask me again, I'm going to TELL you again
See below	I'm not going to give up until you reply
To put it more simply	I clearly need to spell it out in words of one syllable
I see your point	… but I could not care less about it
To clarify	Let me explain it again because you obviously didn't read my last email
Just checking in	You're already a week late, where's my report?

Not sure if my last email reached you?	If you don't answer this time, I'm going to tell your boss
Just looping [boss's name] into the conversation	ESCALATION ALERT
Kind regards	I'm just trying to sound polite
Regards	I'm not even trying to sound polite

EMAIL FAILS

Can you even count yourself a true WFH email veteran if you haven't committed all of these email crimes?

'I'M ATTACHING THE PROPOSAL BELOW.' No, you're not. There's no attachment and you'll have to email everyone saying, 'Haha, oops, I'd forget my own head if it wasn't attached,' but you'll STILL forget to attach the attachment. If you don't manage to send the attachment in the next 17 attempts, either your recipients will find the document themselves on the shared company drive or you'll have to resign in shame, change your name and agree never to use emails ever again.

PRESSING 'REPLY' INSTEAD OF 'FORWARD'. The consequences of this email faux pas range from the mildly embarrassing to the unambiguously career-ending ('Look what [boss's name] just wrote. Ha ha, what a total fool').

SIGNING OFF WITH LOVE AND KISSES. Even if the odd 'x' is appropriate in work emails, if you absentmindedly finish an email with 'lots of love, Jenny xxx', then Phil from Financial Operations may wonder if you're interested in more than just his new invoicing software. Signing off with 'love, Mum' is also usually a no-no unless it's a family business.

PIMP YOUR EMAILS

Sometimes the classic stock phrases we use in our emails can feel a bit passé. If you're getting bored of playing safe with your online correspondence, why not take inspiration from some cultural icons:

* **YODA:** 'Received my last email I hope you have.'
* **DARTH VADER:** 'Your lack of a reply to my recent email disappoints me.'
* **MACBETH:** 'Is this an attachment I see before me? I think you've forgotten to attach it, please can you check and resend?'

* **ALEXANDER HAMILTON:** 'I am not throwing away my mailshot.'
* **DOLLY PARTON:** 'Emailing 9 to 5, what a way to make a living.'
* **MICHAEL CORLEONE:** 'I'll send him an email he can't refuse.'
* **THE TERMINATOR:** 'Hasta la vista, [boss's name].'
* **JANE AUSTEN:** 'It is a truth universally acknowledged that every 20-message email thread could have been a five-minute phone conversation instead.'

UP YOUR ACRONYM GAME

It's important to throw a few acronyms into conversation to really keep your colleagues on their toes and make them feel out of the loop on the most up-to-date WFH slang. Here are a few suggestions to get you started:

OMG = online meetings, great
BTW = blame the Wi-Fi
WTH = where's the host?
ILU = I love unmuting
TGIF = trousers? gosh, I forgot
SMH = someone's mansplaining, help
IDC = I don't conference-call
SMS = silent microphone situation
DM = decline meeting
BRB = burp, reallocate blame

ONLINE SURVEILLANCE

Some companies are so concerned we're not working hard enough from our homes that they're installing additional software into our computers to keep tabs on us during the day. While we may not be able to switch these creepy features off completely, we can at least play our bosses at their own game. Our handy 'anti-sneak kit' will keep you in control, and allow you to take as many long loo breaks as you want.

* If your bosses are keeping count of your keystrokes, bribe one of your children (or a bored housemate) to sit at your computer hammering the keys in a random order. Think of it as substitute piano practice – much quieter than the real thing, so your neighbours will thank you.

* If your camera has been hijacked to monitor your presence at your desk, set up a projector behind your laptop screen and put a white screen where you normally sit, then beam a film of you typing, wearing headphones, looking interested and saying, 'Great idea, Jan, let's do that' at random intervals.

* If your computer windows are being viewed by management, set up a slide-show of snaps from last year's summer party, featuring shots of your boss sliding under the table after too many flaming sambucas. With a little luck and persistence, you should find Board Policy on computer surveillance shifting to a less intrusive method.

PRODUCTIVITY SCHMODUCTIVITY

Remember when people used to talk about 'work–life balance' like it was actually a thing? De-stressing experts would tell us to 'leave work at work' and have a 'coming-home routine' to help us leave the cares of the work day behind. Well, that kind of talk was all very well in the Before Times, but now that our offices are in our kitchens, living rooms and bedrooms, it can be hard knowing where work ends and life begins.

DANGER SIGNS THAT WORK HAS TAKEN OVER YOUR ENTIRE LIFE

★ You regularly schedule meetings for when you're in the bath, calling on your rubber duckies to provide back-up for your more ambitious strategy ideas.

* You make yourself a phone-holder headband so you can video-conference colleagues while getting the children ready for school, making dinner or going for a run.
* You refer to the weekly shopping list as the 'Food Agenda', and when your family members want to ask you a question you tell them to save it for AOB.
* All household members are required to refer to you as 'the CEO', and the evening's TV viewing choices have to be decided by a complex and much-disputed series of email polls.
* You keep referring to your children as 'the interns' and calling their pocket money 'subsistence expenses'. You base your decisions about their Christmas presents on how closely their naughty:nice ratio matches up to their performance objectives for the year.

THERE'S NO PLACE LIKE WORK

COMPARING WORK DISTRACTIONS BEFORE AND AFTER THE WFH ERA

BEFORE	AFTER
Check the post when it arrives. An invoice? Better pass it to Accounts.	Check the post when it arrives. New shoes? Great! Let me try them on. Now let me see how they go with a different outfit. This would be perfect for Instagram. Better upload it.
Gossip in the kitchen at break times.	Make yourself snacks literally all the time, while WhatsApping your friends about how bored and stressed you are.

Discreetly ogle the good-looking window cleaner.	Discreetly ogle the good-looking window cleaner (and then pay them for cleaning your windows, as your boss refuses to do this for you now you're WFH, quite unfairly).

HOW TO DECIDE IF IT'S TIME FOR A BREAK

Have you done at least five minutes' work? Then it's time to take a break. You don't want to overdo things. WFH burnout is *real*.

HOW TO LOOK PRODUCTIVE WHILE WFH

Nobody really knows how much you're getting done every day, spyware excepted, so the most important thing is to at least *appear* to be productive, using these handy tips:

Leave your jacket on the back of your chair during whole-company Zoom meetings to show you'll 'be back any moment'.

Type out draft email replies ('Thanks for the info – noted' is a classic) and schedule them to be sent at various times during the day, leaving you free to take a nap or catch up with your Netflix commitments.

Arrange for a friend to phone you during a particularly tedious work meeting, look at the phone screen, say, 'Sorry, it's a customer – I'm going to have to take this one' to your colleagues, and then never return to the meeting.

Remember not to live-tweet about what's on TV during said meeting.

Also try to avoid chilling out in any parks close to your boss or your work rival's homes – you don't want to have to jump into a bush if you suddenly see them.

'NO, IT ONLY LOOKS LIKE I'M ASLEEP, HONEST'

You've been concentrating all day – well, almost all day – well, for at least a few minutes – look, it's been a long day, all right? And now your boss has sprung a 5 p.m. team meeting on you. Yes, it's a breach of the Geneva Convention, but no, there's probably not much you can do about it right now. Here's what you're going to need to get through it.

Notepad and pen so you can doodle to keep yourself awake

Mug of wine (with taped-on teabag tag for added *authenticité* – just be careful to do any refills off-camera)

Second screen behind your work screen, showing your current favourite series

Earpods (making you look hyper-professional though you're actually listening to the show on your second screen)

Multiple tabs open so you can commentate on your boss's boring voice to your friends (just don't do it on the meeting's chat window as that usually doesn't end well)

"I LOVE TO BRAINSTORM NEW IDEAS IN MY CHILL-OUT ZONE.

THE

BED

WITH MY EYES SHUT."

THE LUNCH
BREAK COMETH

After a hard morning's graft at the deskface, with only three coffee breaks (plus walking the dog, letting the cat out and then in again, and checking social media fifteen times), it's time to give yourself a well-earned break. WFH lunch breaks are different from office-based ones – for a start, nobody will notice if you're not back at your desk exactly one hour after you left to buy an overpriced sandwich which you then ate sitting on a damp park bench – but they're just as important for your wellbeing.

With a little ingenuity you can squeeze in a nutritionally balanced meal (we may not be the first to say this, but a hot dog in each hand *is* a balanced meal), some exercise and some fun as well. Just try to make it back to your laptop before your 2 p.m. catch-up with your manager – and check your chin for ketchup splashes beforehand to be on the safe side.

PROS AND CONS OF LFH (LUNCHING FROM HOME)

PROS

- ★ Never having to wait for the microwave to be free (unless your housemate is selfishly using it).
- ★ Not having to smell someone else's tuna bake for the rest of the afternoon (with the above caveat regarding housemates).
- ★ Never being forced to listen to your colleague's fascinating monologue on the benefits of the 5:2 diet or how happy they feel since they gave up carbs (a lie).

CONS

- ★ No unexpected biscuits or cake unless you bought them yourself and then had an attack of amnesia (or your housemate wants to say sorry for the tuna smell permeating the house).
- ★ You're unlikely to be invited out somewhere fancy for lunch by your boss (though,

depending on your relationship with your boss, this could be a pro).

★ If you find yourself getting enraged at the state of the microwave or the pile of dishes in the sink, there's probably no one to blame but yourself. Try writing a strongly worded email to yourself about this afterwards – you will undoubtedly feel better.

★ The rota for buying new milk for the office fridge probably only has your name on it, and if the milk kitty is empty then it's you that'll have to cough up for it. Again.

DINE LIKE A LORD (OR A MIDDLE-RANKING OFFICE WORKER)

Now that you're WFH you can have pretty much anything you want for lunch, as long as you can rustle it up in your kitchen (which is, conveniently, also your office now). But beware – if any online meetings spill into your break time your lunch choices may send unintended messages about you:

WHAT YOU'RE EATING	WHAT YOUR COLLEAGUES ARE THINKING
Caviar on toast	'Are they paying you more than me?'
Microwave meal eaten directly from the container	'What a lazy …'
Roast dinner	'We all know your mum just delivered that. (Can I come round next time? Please?)'
Entire packet of chocolate biscuits	'Good to see someone who can focus on a task and see it through to the end.'
Whole can of beans on toast	'Actually it's probably best that you're WFH today.'

"HEY, SHIRLEY, I REALLY LIKE THE DECORATION ON YOUR T-SHIRT! OH, THOSE ARE CRISP CRUMBS? LOVE THE WAY YOU'RE STYLING THEM."

SET UP YOUR OWN FUN ZONE

Where your old office had a ping-pong table and a vending machine, you'll need your own WFH amusement zone so you can hang out and bond with your colleagues (OK, with your housemates, pets or, failing that, your teddybear). Try these suggestions for size:

★ **SWINGBALL POST:** if you don't have an outdoor space for this, position it somewhere where breakages are acceptable, e.g. your flatmate's bedroom.

★ **GAMES CONSOLE:** running around shooting bad guys is a great way to relieve stress after a hard morning of departmental meetings. Just remember you can't zap the baddies at work. Unfortunately.

★ **DARTBOARD:** you don't have to put the face of your most annoying top brass or least favourite customer on it, but we won't judge you if you do.

BUILDING EXERCISE INTO YOUR LUNCH BREAK

After giving your little grey cells a workout all morning, your body will be wanting some exercise too. Just try not to move too suddenly after being cocooned on your sofa in a slanket* all morning – you don't want to pull a muscle, as the afternoon's online meetings are likely to be painful enough already without you having a cricked neck, or a bag of frozen peas strapped to your elbow.

These exercise ideas should invigorate your fitness routine, leaving you refreshed and raring to go for the rest of the day.

If it's raining, or you're so committed to the no-trousers way of life that going outside isn't really an option, set yourself a series of indoor Olympic challenges:

* Sleeved blanket. If you haven't invested in one already, please take a moment to question all of your life choices up to this point.

* **PEA SHOOTING:** another great use for those frozen peas, and your pet will have something interesting to hunt for afterwards.
* **STAIRS BOBSLEIGH:** make sure you've borrowed the mattresses from everyone's beds and padded the hallways at the bottom of the stairs before launching yourself on your world-record-breaking descent. If you're using a communal staircase outside your flat for this, it's probably a good idea to wear trousers.
* **PEN JAVELIN:** see how far you can launch your pen down the hallway, as you visualise bringing down a galloping bison with your mighty spear or impaling the head of HR who turned down your last request for a pay rise.

On sunny days, and for those of us who are prepared to don trousers, the local park offers numerous sporting possibilities to get you ready for the afternoon:

* A long-distance run
* A game of five-a-side football
* Parkour

Just kidding. Unless you're a nutter who loves to jog, a wannabe professional footballer or a teenager who loves breaking bones, we know you'd much rather stay in and focus on being trouserless.

HOW TO TURN YOUR LUNCH BREAK INTO A MINI VACATION

You may not be having a real holiday any time soon, so build a little time into your lunch break for a VFH: a Vacation From Home.

Set up a projector in your bathroom showing tropical scenes, put on your best bikini and turn your bath into an infinity pool. (Just try not to flood the flat downstairs.)

Wear a straw hat and a Hawaiian shirt while drinking your post-lunch coffee out of a hollowed-out pineapple. In this era of trouserlessness, Bermuda shorts are optional.

Print out famous artworks and pin them to your hallway walls, then spend a whole hour walking up and down looking at them, taking wonky photos and uploading them to Instagram with the hashtags #artgallery #culture #myfeethurt. Look in your last holiday bag for a €10 note to spend on a small panini afterwards, to complete the experience.

Wearing mirror shades and those sports sandals you once bought under the influence of New Year's Resolution optimism, climb the stairs, then turn round at the top to admire the view, proclaiming loudly, 'The air is so much fresher at these heights!' Take a proud selfie to mark your ascent of Mount Myhouse.

CALMING YOGA POSES TO DE-STRESS YOU

When you're back at your desk and are ready to get back to work, you can still keep your body aligned and at peace with a series of yoga moves. This often fits nicely with the demands of the working day.

POSITION		WHAT IT MEANS
Cobra		I am paying attention
Down dog		I may or may not be paying attention
Triangle		I have an idea
Chair		Please buy me an office chair, just look at me for goodness sake
Seated crossed-legged, eyes closed		I actually concentrate better with my eyes closed
Child's pose		Just taking a little nap
Corpse pose		We are done here, I'm out

SERVING LOOKS

(PYJAMAS ARE A LOOK)

One of the very best things about working from home is that you can wear whatever you like and no one will judge you, below the waist at least. Everywhere north of the place where you used to wear a belt (back in those historical times when you wore trousers almost every day) might need to look professional from time to time, but never fear: as long as you're still trouserless, the spirit of WFH will be strong in you.

'I USED TO *WEAR* THAT???'

Trousers are not the only item of clothing that WFH-ers can jettison from their work wardrobes forever. Languishing alongside our suit trousers, work slacks and non-stretch jeans (what were we *thinking*?), the office-dress archaeologists of the future will find thick strata of other unworn garments:

* **BRAS:** with no colleagues to judge us for swinging free, we can breathe in peace, and the only place you'll find underwires is lying forgotten under our beds, gathering dust.
* **TIGHTS:** no need to be squeezed in nylon sausage casings all day any more (though we'll keep those nice thick baggy ones for trouserless chilly days).

* **HIGH HEELS:** from now on our shoe choices fall into two clear categories – slippers for indoors and trainers for everywhere else.
* **TIES:** male office staff may need to look smart from time to time but everyone has their limit, and silk nooses are out *forever*.
* **SHAPEWEAR:** remember Spanx? Remember caring about belly rolls? My WFH body has a shape, thank you very much, and if that shape is squishy and rolly then it's going to be that way in peace.
* **BELTS:** if you never wear trousers, you'll never need anything to hold them up. Simples.

WFH DRESS-DOWN FRIDAYS

Some traditions are too important to be broken, and the office institution of dress-down Friday is one of these. Since every day is dressed down now, thanks to the more relaxed setting of WFH life, we're going to have to mix things up a bit to make the most of our Friday freedom. Here are a few ideas:

Swapping your everyday 'work' slippers for more outlandish 'fun' slippers on Fridays. If you normally rock a pair of fluffy bunny slippers during the week, how about switching up to unicorn heads or monster feet to celebrate the imminent arrival of the weekend?

Celebrate a week of not wearing any trousers by not wearing any pants on Fridays. (Double-checking your camera angles is advised here.)

Dress as your hero (from the waist up, of course). A Neil Armstrong costume complete with helmet will give you an excuse not to hear your boss's ideas at the end-of-week briefing; the twinkling rhinestones on your Elvis jacket will distract people from focusing too closely on your presentation to the board; and your Anna Wintour shades will let you take a quick nap during the departmental catch-up. Nice! 😎

WFH FASHION INNOVATION: MEN'S EDITION

The top scientists in fashion labs all over the world are probably working on this already, but the question on all WFH men's lips is: 'When are we going to get a WFH Zoom suit?' This handy one-piece pull-on garment will contain all the key elements of formal business wear in a single top-half-only look. You'll slip on a comfy sweatshirt-like item that carefully re-creates the styled lines of a smart suit jacket, button-down shirt and Ralph Lauren silk tie – so that from the waist up you look like the smart executive you've tried to convince your boss you actually are. Come *on*, scientists – we need you!

STYLING YOUR WFH LOOK FROM SEASON TO SEASON

To give yourself a much-needed boost throughout the year, why not invest in a few snazzy seasonal looks for your eyes and comfort only. After all, is there a better way to let loose than purchasing a selection of matching pants and socks?

JANUARY: Glitter and sparkles all the way to celebrate the new year, or (depending on how you're coping with a WFH winter) to cheer you up as you spend the shortest, darkest days staring at your laptop and forgetting what the sun looks like.

FEBRUARY: Hearts and roses for the month of love. If you're feeling romantic, try sending a sockfie showing your Valentine's outfit to the object of your desires.

MARCH: Spring is coming! It's time for floral pant and sock combos, with a frolicking lamb or two if you're feeling really fancy.

APRIL: Who says Easter eggs are only for eating? Put your best foot forward in socks decorated in eggs and bunnies, with matching pants, of course.

MAY: Spend all month dancing with a maypole-patterned lower half. And when Eurovision comes round, you know it's time to crack out your Waterloo set of Benny and Björn pants with Anni-Frid and Agnetha socks.

JUNE: Summer is here at last. Even if you're stuck inside staring at a spreadsheet, your pants and socks can display a fine range of ice creams, sunglasses and palm trees. So relaxing!

JULY: Wimbledon season – if you're sporty, rock some thick white socks with your tighty-whities, while if you're more of a spectator, your socks and pants will be covered in tennis rackets and strawberries – and maybe an umbrella or two as well, to be on the safe side.

AUGUST: Everyone's on holiday, so you can try going without any socks and pants at all if you like. (Just make sure the neighbours don't have a good view of your pantless WFH setup.)

SEPTEMBER: The leaves are starting to turn golden, so it's the perfect moment to dress yourself in falling-leaf pants with acorn-patterned socks.

OCTOBER: Your colleagues may be keeping their lower halves secret, but you just *know* that, like you, they're rocking an awesome sock-and-pant set bedecked with pumpkins, skeletons and spooky spiders.

NOVEMBER: Start your month with a bang, cladding yourself in the finest firework-themed accessories for your feet and nether regions. Just don't ask any of your colleagues if they want to see your Roman Candle – trust us, they really don't.

DECEMBER: Jingle socks, jingle socks, jingle all the way! Make sure your socks and pants are covered in Santas, snowmen and Christmas trees, and you'll have the best WFH festive season *ever*.

GETTING FANCY

There are some days when the same old same old just won't cut it, and you want to show your colleagues that you're still a fashion-forward jetsetter on the looks front. If your colleagues see you modelling any of the following beauty techniques, they'll know you mean business – so use your power wisely.

SIGNS YOU'RE AT THE TOP OF THE WFH BEAUTY GAME

* You brushed your hair this morning.
* You know where your hairbrush actually is.
* You're wearing make-up. Yes, that eyeliner may be a bit Picasso-esque, but you made an effort – and that's what counts.
* Your eyebrows are two separate items of face furniture and you can't plait them (or hardly, anyway).
* Your T-shirt is ironed.
* You're wearing matching socks. Or any socks at all.

WHO WEARS THE
TROUSERS
ROUND HERE?

NOT ME!

NEVER WFH
WITH CHILDREN ...

It can be difficult sharing a working space with people who make unreasonable demands on your time, express themselves through temper tantrums and don't know how to flush the toilet. But now that you're working from home you don't have to spend time with those idiots any more – you've got your kids for company instead.

OUT OF THE MOUTHS OF BABES AND TEENAGERS

If there's one thing children are really good at, it's saying what they think, very loudly, without stopping to consider the possible consequences. This is great much of the time, especially when furnishing you with hilarious stories to tell your long-suffering friends and

relatives, but in virtual meetings it can lead to the
occasional awkward silence.

TOP TEN USEFUL MEETING CONTRIBUTIONS FROM CHILDREN

* 'Oh yes, he *is* really bald, just like you said!'
* 'Daddy, where are your trousers?'
* 'Is that the Big Meanie?'
* 'Mummy, I thought you said the evil lady was on holiday this week? Why can I see her on your screen?'
* 'Did you just fart? *Somebody* just farted – and it wasn't me.'
* 'Which one is the Pain in the Neck, Mummy?'
* 'Your boss does have a funny voice! Can you do it for us like you did last night?'
* 'I drew a picture of you and Mummy in bed – shall I show it to everyone?'
* 'I'm going to do a poo. Look! I did it!'
* 'Why are you working today? Normally we go to the park in the afternoons, don't we?'

NOT FORGETTING NON-VERBAL CONTRIBUTIONS ...

As well as providing helpful suggestions during meetings, children are often willing to create a relaxing workplace soundscape, including loud crashes, bangs and howls. Somehow they seem to have a sixth sense enabling them to create the most intense walls of sound during your career-making-or-breaking presentation to the board. Possible solutions include noise-cancelling headphones, a lock on your office door (on the inside, of course) and boarding school.

DID I REALLY JUST SAY THAT?

Living with children can have an impact on a parent's vocabulary, all the more so when the only people you see from day to day are people of school age and your partner (who's in the same Stockholm-syndrome boat as you).

As a result of spending all day every day with small people, you may hear yourself saying any of the following:

* 'I'm sorry, Ralph's started eating the cat's food – I'll be back in a minute.'
* 'Mummy's in a meeting, darling – can't you play on the iPad a bit longer? Or how about watching some more cartoons?'
* 'Please don't stick those up your nose – oh no, not again …'
* 'Not now, Daddy needs a number two – I'll be there in a minute.'
* 'Yes, you can have another biscuit, but PLEASE leave me in peace for five minutes for GOD'S SAKE.'
* 'PUT YOUR SISTER DOWN! NO, I DID NOT MEAN DROP YOUR SISTER. SAY SORRY.'
* 'If you can't share then you're not having any Xbox time at all.'
* 'Let's play "Who can be quiet for the longest?", shall we?'

No need to feel embarrassed if you say any of these during virtual meetings: your fellow parents will sympathise, and the non-parents will have something more entertaining to enjoy than Derek's quarterly accounts PowerPoint slides.

HOME OFFICE, HOME SCHOOL, HOME EVERYTHING

Working from home with kids can sometimes lead you into a double life. Not only are you a professional executive who gets results and expects top performance, you're also a full-time childminder and home educator. Lucky you – you're so versatile! And those extra wrinkles and grey hairs you've gained make you look really distinguished.

Obviously, when you become a home-schooler your respect for what teachers achieve every day increases a thousand-fold – but then, when you consider that teachers are working in an actual *school*, that they've been *professionally trained*, and that *nobody's expecting*

'HONESTLY, MY COLLEAGUES ARE JUST LIKE FAMILY TO ME. HANG ON, THEY ARE MY FAMILY.'

them to write a 32-page strategy report for Head Office while teaching, you'd be forgiven for wondering who has the tougher deal.

For a synergistic win—win that will tick off key educational milestones while also helping you get your job done, try out our new WFH school syllabus.

GEOGRAPHY: 'Where in the world have I left those figures for this afternoon's meeting?'

ECONOMICS: If Mummy needs to generate 20 per cent more profit this year, while also having a 30 per cent budget cut, how can she meet her target without having a nervous breakdown?

HUMAN BIOLOGY: Draw a diagram to illustrate what Mummy meant when she said, 'Look, if Sam asks me to produce another 100-slide presentation "just in case" one more time, I'm going to stick his [redacted] up his [redacted] and then he won't be able to [also redacted] for a week.'

HISTORY: When Daddy described last week's company meeting, did he compare it to (a) World War I, (b) World War II or (c) World War III?

PHILOSOPHY: If an email lands in an inbox and no one is around to read it, will anyone ever care?

LANGUAGES: Long-term WFH while also caring for children full-time is likely to acquaint your delicate offspring with a range of Anglo-Saxon words and phrases. Your challenge is to persuade them not to use their new-found vocabulary when Skyping Granny in the evening.

CLIMATE SCIENCE: When toxic gases build up in an enclosed space, the wellbeing of the people in that space is affected. 'Ewwww – was that you or the dog? Quick, open a window, someone.'

PHYSICAL EDUCATION: 'Honestly, I've had enough of this. Let's go and play in the park for a bit.'

... OR ANIMALS

One of the nicest things about WFH is that your furry/feathery/scaly friends can spend the day with you, instead of having to wait at home chewing the furniture while you're out.

MEET YOUR NEW WFH COLLEAGUES

Aside from any other actual humans who might be sharing your working space (children, partner, flatmate, the builders next door who might as well be in your home for all the noise they're making), you don't have to feel lonely or starved of office companionship. Meet your WFH officemates:

DOG

JOB TITLE: Office counsellor

GOOD POINTS: Always cheerful, wants you to be happy, won't judge you for snacking

BAD POINTS: May attempt to blame own farts on you, will guilt-stare you into sharing your snacks

MOST LIKELY TO BE: Curled up on your feet, sleeping

CAT

JOB TITLE: HR director

GOOD POINTS: Always perfectly turned out, occasionally available to sit on your lap and keep you warm

BAD POINTS: Never praises you for meeting your targets, always looks at dinner as if to say, 'You could do so much better'

MOST LIKELY TO BE: Walking on your keyboard, preferably during a meeting

SPIDER ON THE CEILING (FOR THOSE WHO DON'T HAVE ANY OTHER PETS)

JOB TITLE: Pest-control operative

GOOD POINTS: Keeps corporate espionage (insect variety) under control

BAD POINTS: Sometimes makes you feel as if you're being watched – you are

MOST LIKELY TO BE: Dangling upside-down keeping an eye (or eight eyes) on things

HOUSE PLANT (FOR THOSE WHO DON'T EVEN HAVE A SPIDER)

JOB TITLE: Environmental officer

GOOD POINTS: Literally creates a good working atmosphere just by being there

BAD POINTS: Not a brilliant communicator, tends to fall over when you forget to water it

MOST LIKELY TO BE: Gathering dust and feeling thirsty

WASHING PILE (FOR THOSE WHO – WELL, YOU GET THE PICTURE)

JOB TITLE: Uniform collector

GOOD POINTS: Good at collecting items, not fussy, makes you look positively organised by comparison

BAD POINTS: Keeps taking all your clothes and not giving them back, especially the really comfy ones

MOST LIKELY TO BE: Growing

A HELPING PAW

There are plenty of ways that your pets can help you succeed in your WFH life. For example:

* You can train your dog to bark its head off every time it hears trigger words such as 'spreadsheet', 'touch base' or 'thought shower'. 'So sorry about this, I'm going to have to take

Rufus outside to calm down – can't imagine what's got into him …'

* If you conceal tasty cat treats under your computer keyboard, your cat will jump up on to your desk during meetings to distract everyone with its intense fluffiness.

* Best of all, if you audibly burp, fart or gurgle, you can blame the dog – who will be proud of the accolade. And don't worry if you don't actually own a dog. If people ask to see your non-existent dog, pick up a soft toy and move it around really quickly in front of the screen as if it has a life of its own – they'll definitely be convinced.

GET *DOWN*, SPOT! TECHNIQUES FOR MANAGING YOUR PETS' WORKPLACE PERFORMANCE

Award extra treats to your cat for every day it doesn't bring you a dead mouse while you're working.

If your cat insists on sitting on your computer keyboard, try giving it a spare keyboard of its very own to sit on instead. Your kitty will almost certainly enjoy copying you and will leave you in peace to get on with your work – and if you're really lucky it might even send a few emails for you. Their spelling is bound to be purrfect. Sorry.

Although you obviously don't want your pet dog/mouse/rat/goat to eat your important documents, you could try leaving any papers you really don't want to deal with in a place where they can be nibbled with ease. Then you'll be telling the truth when you say, 'I'm so sorry I haven't read all the documents yet – my dog ate them – yes, I know, would you believe it?!! You couldn't make it up.'

THINKING OUTSIDE THE BARKS

Although cats and dogs are the most popular pets, there's a whole range of more unusual friends just waiting for you to invite them into your family and your next Zoom meeting.

Once you've taken into account the welfare needs of any animal you bring home, you can also consider how each type of pet will enhance your image as a colleague:

* **HEDGEHOG:** prickly – do not mess with – but also unbearably cute. Prefers a 'Do not disturb' strategy for the winter months.
* **PYTHON:** the ultimate shoulder companion in a difficult meeting, very impressive. Will also keep you warm and give you an excuse to put the heating on even if your housemates are insistent that you could wear an extra jumper instead.
* **PIRANHA:** a well-positioned tank of terrifying killer fish will ensure that your request for a pay rise is taken seriously.

* **TORTOISE:** resilient, maybe lacking in 'va-va-voom' but surprisingly nippy (in both senses) when needs must.
* **PARROT:** very useful if you have a mouth like a sailor. 'Sarah, was that you saying, "For f★★★'s sake, not another c★★★ing meeting" just now?' 'Nope, it was my bird. Polly, how could you say that to the CEO? No coconut cubes for you tonight.'
* **GUINEA PIG:** utterly adorable. When perched on your shoulder, nobody will be able to tell you off for missing last month's sales targets because they'll be overwhelmed by the sheer cuteness of your pet's twitchy nose.

THE OFFICE SOCIAL

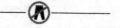

(AKA OBLIGATORY FUN AND HOW TO SURVIVE IT)

At last! It's 6 p.m. (or 5 p.m., or 4 p.m. ... I'm not judging you) and you can switch off your computer, put your feet up and forget about work for the rest of the day ...

RECORD-SCRATCH SOUND EFFECT

Hold on a second – what's that? A ping from your online calendar to alert you to tonight's main event: 'ONLINE FUN WITH THE TEAM, 6 p.m. till late'. Oh great.

Yes, it seems that the powers that be in our various office buildings all over the globe have decided that, after a day of staring at each other on computer screens while we work, what we really need is another couple of hours of staring at each other on computer screens while we play. Yay.

IN QUIZ WE TRUST

Wherever you work, and whatever you do, it is a universal law that when you're embedded into the WFH life, you have to undertake at least one staff pub quiz a month. Being teamed up with our work nemesis to answer questions about the World Snooker Championship of 2013 is the price we pay for never having to see each other in person, it seems.

If you're going to survive the quiz without stabbing yourself in the leg with a fork just to stay awake, these handy tips will help:

Recruit a housemate or family member to
google the quiz answers for you while they're
being read out, so you can have the answers
before anyone else but without any suspicious
'I'm definitely typing during the quiz'

giveaway movements. Try to avoid having an obvious stage-whisper-in-your-ear, or saying 'What was that?' to someone clearly off-screen, to maintain appearances.

Ask the organiser if each department can set its own round of questions, and make sure your own round is focused on in-joke information that nobody else would know. 'What national anthem did Tricia burp for us in our last team catch-up?' is a good one.

Stage a takeover of the quiz, loudly declaring, 'I'm asking the questions here.' The main benefit of this is that you can't lose if you're the quizmaster – and with a little luck you'll have been so disruptive that you'll be barred from all future quizzes.

If all else fails, create a doppelganger for yourself, using a couple of old pillows, some permanent marker and a wig. Prop your new self in front of the computer, message everyone that you've got a sore throat and won't be speaking, and then go and do something more interesting in the other room. Nobody will ever know.

QUIZ ALTERNATIVES

Contrary to most office social event organisers' beliefs, there is more to life than trivia quizzes. Just in case your own imaginative reserves are running low after several months of WFH, our *Compendium of Obligatory Fun Evenings In* is here to guide you.

WFH FILM CLUB

Obviously, the best thing about a work film night is that you don't have to talk to each other during the screening. Ideally your office will send you a supply of microwave popcorn to get you all into the mood. Otherwise you can spend a tenner on a small bag of sweets and a 2-litre cup of Coke to recreate the authentic cinema experience. Here are some suggested genres to go for, depending on the kind of week your team has had:

* **ACTION:** to get everybody riled up for the big pitch next week
* **COMEDY:** to let go after a long week
* **ROMANTIC:** if you know two of your colleagues have feelings for each other but are both too shy to act on them
* **HORROR:** to remind people what could happen if the big pitch flops next week
* **THRILLER:** to help the team think of management's non-stop changes of strategy as an adventure rather than a waking nightmare
* **PERIOD DRAMA:** to remind everybody what good manners look like

WFH PARTY GAMES CHANGED FOR REMOTE WORKING

For a dose of true party atmosphere, try introducing children's games into your WFH socials. With a little luck there will be tears before the end and someone's parents will be called to take them home early. (If you're really lucky it'll be you.) The hottest tips on the WFH Party Games agenda are:

* **PASS THE ELECTRONIC PARCEL:** This game involves sending an attachment round a group of players, with each player making a change and saving the file name in their own unique way, creating a file called something like 'Final File+jenny+draft 2+edit_FINAL+changes 1.3_FINISHED.doc'. By the end of each round you should have a file that nobody is sure whether to use or not. Most office workers will be advanced gamers already. It doesn't really matter how you score this round as it's a game nobody can win.

* **MUSICAL CHAIRS:** For this game, everyone dances on their own in front of their Zoom screens, and when the party organiser stops the music, your housemate, responding to a secret message from the organiser, may or may not snatch your desk chair away just as you try to sit down. The winner is the last person sitting,

and the losers all now have a grudge against their housemates.

★ **THE TELEPHONE GAME:** This is a well-known game played every day in most organisations, but in order to play it at a social event the organiser calls a player and explains a complicated strategy, such as a complete reorganisation of all the desks in the office. Players take it in turns to call each other to pass the message on, with the final player calling the organiser to explain that the office is being relocated to Mars and the main conference room will be a bouncy castle.

★ **CONSEQUENCES:** Although indulging in speculation about our colleagues is another daily office sport, the online party version of this requires each participant to provide a specific piece of information with no context, to produce the following type of story: [colleague 1's name] met [colleague 2's name] at [place] to [reason for being there]; Colleague 1 said [what they said] and Colleague 2 [did something], and the consequence was [what happened]. Played as a truly random game, this can be a lot of fun, but can produce stories along the lines of '[boss's name] met [staff member's name] in the [stationery cupboard] at [last year's Christmas party] and […]', so you may need to be prepared for awkwardness and/or finding a new job. At least WFH has saved us all from this year's Christmas party. Unless … it goes … online …

OTHER ONLINE SOCIAL ACTIVITIES

THE GREAT OFFICE BAKE OFF: The only cake you can taste is your own, and you can judge everyone else's based on appearances. The good news is that you get to eat your entire cake by yourself. The bad news is that your underwear waistband was already getting tight – time to do some late-night ordering again.

FANCY DRESS COMPETITION: Prizes for the most imaginative, most terrifying and most like the CEO (just don't let the CEO win that one or they'll get big-headed). Remember: fancy dress from the waist up only – we're still playing by WFH rules.

CRAZY GOLF: Each player builds themselves a course from piled-up work folders (Ah! So *that* was why you needed to bring them home), with jam jars to catch the balls. Then, using a rolled-up copy of your work contract, compete with your colleagues to pot the most balls/cause the most damage to your WFH space. If you manage to smash your webcam while playing, not only do you get a bonus point but you don't have to finish the game. Winning!

THE WFH COCKTAIL CABINET

Online social events are not always quite as much fun as your boss would like them to be, so you may find yourself reaching for some alcoholic refreshment to keep you going. Here are some drinking-from-home cocktails, with notes on how they are vital to the WFH lifestyle to help you choose your go-to beverage:

* **BLOODY MARY:** What you say when your colleague who promised to be your wingwoman at tonight's tedious quiz didn't show up.
* **LONG ISLAND ICED TEA:** Useful for drinking at all times of day – after all, it's 'tea', isn't it, and it's always time for tea in the office. *HIC*
* **MANHATTAN:** Somewhere you dream of visiting instead of staring at your living-room walls and the bottomless pit of unending online meetings.
* **MARGARITA:** Useful reminder to order pizzas for dinner tonight.

* **COSMOPOLITAN:** What you used to be, back in those days when you wore trousers and left the house every day for exotic events called 'meetings' and 'conferences'.
* **TOM COLLINS:** Some random guy who crashed your last Zoom meeting and showed everyone he wasn't wearing any trousers.
* **MOSCOW MULE:** IT keeps warning you about these, but to be quite honest your emails aren't interesting enough to hack.
* **SCREWDRIVER:** Handy if your homemade desk starts wobbling.
* **TEQUILA SUNRISE:** Only experienced after an exceptionally rowdy all-night office party.
* **PORN STAR MARTINI:** When you accidentally share your OnlyFans page during a meeting and reveal your outside-work-hours alter ego.

EXCUSE ME

However willing you are to be a good sport and support your boss's inexplicable compulsion to unite the team through online trivia quizzes, there will come a night when the very IDEA of spending a MILLISECOND more of your PRECIOUS TIME with your colleagues seems utterly insupportable. You'll need a good excuse, because 'the quiz team just isn't the same without you', apparently. Try one of these for size:

* 'Oh, I have a call with [important person from an office on a different continent], so I won't be able to join you, I'm afraid.' Galaxy-brain variant of this: get your international colleague on board with an alibi, so you can offer them the same favour another time.
* 'My internet gets switched off at 6 p.m. every day – so weird, I know!'
* 'I'm sorry, Philippa is giving a mandolin recital in the online school concert tonight and I really can't miss this one.'

* ~~'I would literally rather stick pins in my eyeballs than spend a second longer with you than I'm being paid for.'~~ Honesty isn't always the best policy, unless it's your last day and you already have a good reference from someone else.
* [shaking your laptop vigorously and looking worried] 'Wow, what's that – some kind of tremor?? I think we're having a very localised earthquake – better check it out.'
* [carefully position your computer screen upside down] 'So weird – looks like the gravity has gone haywire??? Going to have to look into this one.'

AFTERWORD

WHEN YOU'RE BACK IN
THE OFFICE ...

Working life has changed for millions of us all over the world, and things will never be the same again. WFH used to be a rare treat, reserved for coping with the boiler engineer's visit or focusing on an important project. Following the events of 2020, untold numbers of us can work from home, even when there's nobody who needs to be let in and nothing serious that needs to be done – apart from gamely attempting to clear our inboxes (it was Sisyphus who invented email, surely).

But one day a message will come from Head Office saying it's time to leave our sofa sanctuaries and return to the mothership, whether it's only one day a week or (heaven forbid) full-time. Why would they want to wrench us out of our cosy dens? It just doesn't seem fair. Maybe they want to check we still have lower halves, or find out if we can communicate face to face like civilised human beings ...

However tough it feels, we're going to have to play along with the bosses a little and give them some face time that isn't FaceTime. Brace yourselves:

IT'S TIME TO PUT YOUR TROUSERS BACK ON

Wow, that hit home. Where *are* my trousers? I suppose I've got these baggy jogging bottoms – will they do? What do you mean, no? Ughhhhhh ... OK then.

The trousers are on, and it's time to rediscover the outside world, a proper desk and chair, and actual colleagues with legs and feet. Here are a few tips to help with the re-entry process:

- ★ Remember, you can't mute other people when they're droning on and on (though you can still tune out and think about something else with a fascinated expression on your face).
- ★ You can't mute yourself either – so it's back to silent burping and farting where possible. 💨
- ★ You don't have to ask to share your screen – your colleagues are right there, they can see your screen if it's pointing at them. (Just make sure you've closed down any sites you don't want them to see.)
- ★ You can't switch off your laptop to make your colleagues go away (boo), but you can literally leave the office at the end of the day and you

won't have to see them again till tomorrow (yay!).

* You don't need to wave at the end of meetings.

Good luck, fellow WFH-er! Remember, even if they force us to wear trousers, there will always be a place for WFH in our hearts. We've got this. Now, where *did* I leave my trousers …?

(I really want to go home now, thanks)

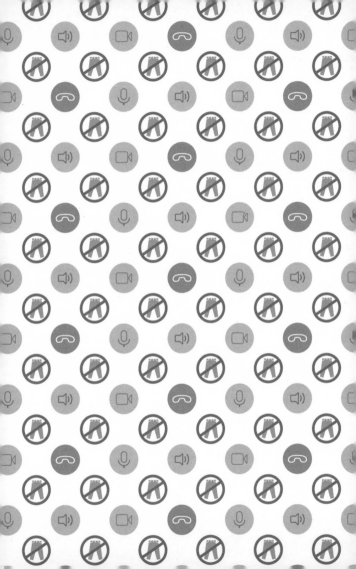